SCHIRMER'S LIBRARY
OF MUSICAL CLASSICS

Vol. 233

LUDWIG van BEETHOVEN

Op. 61

Concerto
In D
For Violin and Piano

With Cadenzas by
HENRY SCHRADIECK

ISBN 978-0-7935-4870-5

G. SCHIRMER, Inc.

DISTRIBUTED BY

HAL•LEONARD®
CORPORATION
7777 W. BLUEMOUND RD. P.O. BOX 13819 MILWAUKEE, WI 53213

To STEPHAN von BREUNING.

Concerto
for the Violin,

with Accompaniment of Orchestra.

L. van BEETHOVEN. Op. 61.
(Composed in 1806.)

To Mr. GUSTAV SCHIRMER.

Cadenzas for Beethoven's Violin Concerto.

For the 1st Movement.

HENRY SCHRADIECK.

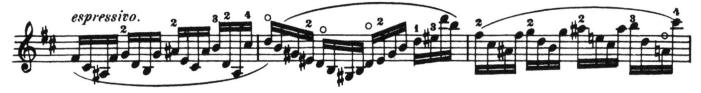

For the 2nd Movement.

For the last Movement.

To STEPHAN von BREUNING.

Concerto
for the Violin,
with Accompaniment of Orchestra.

Violin.

L. van BEETHOVEN. Op. 61.
(Composed in 1806.)

Allegro, ma non troppo.

Violin.

Violin.

6 **Violin.**

Violin.

Violin.

Violin.

Violin.

Violin.

Violin.

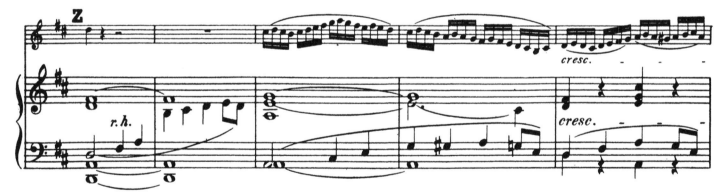

Larghetto.

Attacca subito il Rondo

Rondo.